Accidental Genius

Science Puzzles for Clever Kids

Meerkats, Snakes, Camels, and Aardvarks

The Desert Biome

Alix Wood

WINDMILL BOOKS

Published in 2024 by Windmill Books,
an Imprint of Rosen Publishing
2544 Clinton Street
Buffalo, NY 14224

Written, designed and illustrated by Alix Wood
All other images © AdobeStock Images

Cataloging-in-Publication Data

Names: Wood, Alix.
Title: Meerkats, snakes, camels, and aardvarks: the desert biome / Alix Wood.
Description: Buffalo, New York : Windmill Books, 2024. | Series: Accidental genius | Includes glossary and index.
Identifiers: ISBN 9781538394816 (pbk.) | ISBN 9781538394823 (library bound) | ISBN 9781538394830 (ebook)
Subjects: LCSH: Desert ecology--Juvenile literature | Games--Juvenile literature. | Picture puzzles--Juvenile literature.
Classification: LCC QH541.5.D4 W66 2024 | DDC 577.54--dc23

Printed in the United States of America

CPSIA Compliance Information: Batch CSWM24
For Further Information contact Rosen Publishing at 1-800-237-9932

Find us on

Contents

What Is a Desert?

Have you ever been to a desert? They are the driest places on Earth. A desert biome gets less than 10 inches (25.4 cm) of rain a year. Not all deserts are hot, bare, and sandy. Some are rocky, with a few scattered plants. A few can even be icy cold!

What are biomes? Biomes are areas with similar weather and temperature. Each type of biome is home to the plants and animals that can survive in those conditions.

Can you find another lizard hiding in this picture?

Where Are Earth's Deserts?

Nearly 20 percent of the land on Earth is desert. On this map, we have colored the hot deserts yellow and the cold deserts light blue. Copy this map, then color the rest of the land in green and the oceans in dark blue.

Color It In

Copy or print this picture if you are sharing this book.

How Are Deserts Made?

Many deserts are near the equator. The equator is an imaginary line around the center of Earth. It is closest to the sun as the Earth spins. The air is very dry there.

Mountains can create deserts, too. The mountains keep rain from reaching the other side.

Deserts can form in the middle of a continent. By the time the wind gets there, it has lost its wetness.

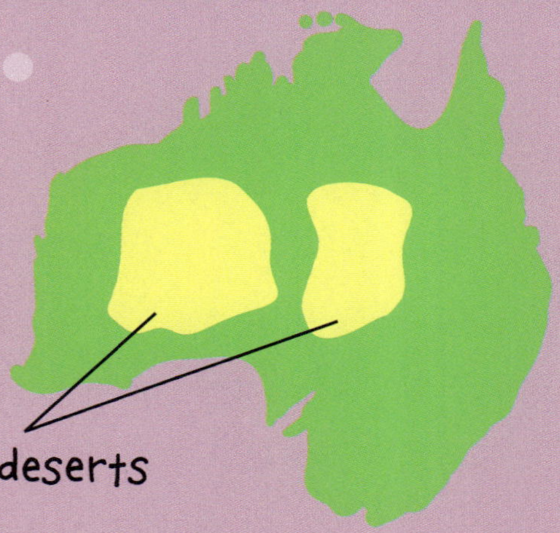

Make Your Own Rain!

You could try this trick in your yard!

1. Dig a hole in the sand. Put a cup in the hole.

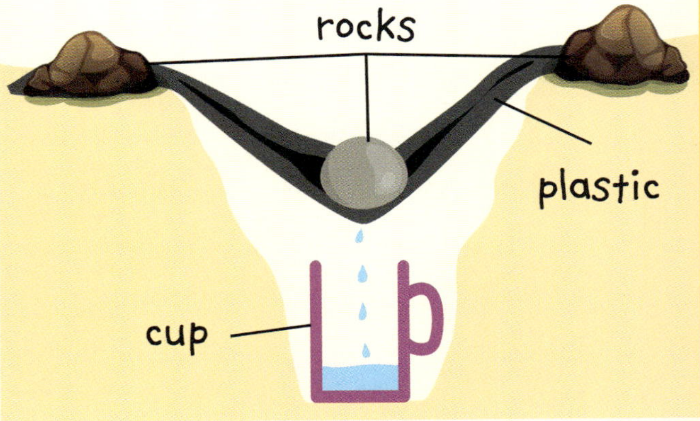

2. Place a sheet of plastic over the hole, held in place with two rocks. Place a third rock on the plastic, over the cup.

3. After a few hours under the hot sun, any water in the air will form droplets on the sheet. Drips will be caught in the cup.

Did you know that deserts can flood? Desert soil is sandy. It doesn't have much clay or plant roots to hold onto any water. So, when it does rain, water doesn't soak into the ground. It flows down slopes and can cause dangerous floods!

Hot Days. . .

Deserts are hottest in the daytime. The temperature can often be over 100° Fahrenheit (38° Celsius) in summer. The world's largest hot, dry desert is the Sahara in North Africa. The Sahara is a sandy desert with giant dunes.

Dry, sandy deserts like the Sahara get very hot. The sun beats down on the sand all day. There are few plants or clouds to create shade. Most plants cannot survive the heat, sandy soil, and lack of water.

What Animals Live in the Sahara?

Which two of these animals would definitely NOT survive in a hot, dry desert?

Strong winds blow loose sand to form the sand dunes.

Where in this picture might an animal find a little shade?

. . .and Cold Nights

Even the hottest deserts can get very cold at night. Deserts have clear, cloudless skies. The sun beats down in the daytime. At night, most of the hot air escapes. There are no clouds to hold the heat in.

Away from the desert, rain clouds act a little like a blanket in the sky. They protect us from the sun's heat in the daytime. They hold hot air below them at night.

The dorcas gazelle keeps cool by looking for its food at night. It can live its whole life without drinking! It gets water from the leaves and flowers it eats.

Color It In

Connect the Dots

Use tracing paper to connect the dots and see what a dorcas gazelle looks like. Then color it!

Where Is the Largest Desert?

Clue 1: It is home to penguins.
Clue 2: It is covered in ice.
Clue 3: It contains the South Pole.

The answer is upside down below.

Answer: Amazingly, Antarctica is the largest desert on Earth! It hardly ever rains or snows there. Antarctica is covered in ice, but the weather is so cold the ice never melts. Scientists believe that in some areas, it hasn't snowed or rained for 14 million years!

Night Life

Many desert animals only come out at night, when it is cool. Animals active at night are called "nocturnal." They are specially adapted to life in the dark.

In daytime, sand cats shelter underground. The sun is coming up. Can you help this sand cat find its burrow?

Shining Eyes

Have you ever noticed that cats' eyes flash brightly at night? Nocturnal animals have special eyes that let in more light than ours. Their eyes reflect light back from flashlights and car headlights.

Waiting for Rain

Toads are amphibians. That means they spend the first part of their lives in water. Does it sound like a desert probably isn't the best home for a toad? Amazingly, the Couch's spadefoot toad manages to make it work!

The Speedy Life Cycle of a Desert Toad

Usually, toads' eggs take about 10 days to hatch and three months to turn into toadlets. Why do you think this spadefoot toad does it so quickly?

Can you put the toad's life cycle stages in the right order from 1 to 3?

Write your answers on a separate sheet of paper.

Ships of the Desert

In the Sahara, people use camels as transport. They are perfectly suited to the hot, sandy desert. They only need to drink every few days. They can go for long periods without food, too.

Camels move both legs on the same side of their body when they walk. They rock from side to side, which makes them quite uncomfortable to ride!

Color It In

Copy or trace this picture if you are sharing this book. Then color it!

Desert Plants

With so little water, how do plants survive in the desert? Some desert plants grow very wide or deep roots to find water. Others store water in their stems, leaves, or trunks.

Match each cactus to its shadow.

Write your answers on a separate sheet of paper.

How Does a Waxy Coating Help a Cactus?

You will need: paper towel, waxed paper, scissors, some water, two clothespins

1. Cut a square of waxed paper the same size as one sheet of paper towel.
2. Dampen two sheets of paper towel. Lay one sheet on top of your waxed paper square.
3. Roll the paper towel into a sausage. Roll the waxed paper towel into a second sausage and fasten both ends with a clothespin. Leave in a warm place overnight.

In the morning, unroll the towels. Are they both damp? Did the waxy coat stop the water from evaporating?

Dust Storms

Desert winds can create huge dust storms. The sky gets thick with dust. It is hard to see or breathe. The strong wind can move huge sand dunes. It can even blow desert dust clouds across the ocean!

Coping with Dust Storms

W	E	T	A	K	R	E	E	M	E
L	I	P	N	S	G	B	U	L	C
E	S	N	R	N	C	X	R	C	R
C	F	E	D	T	H	E	R	A	E
S	A	N	D	S	T	O	R	M	S
A	D	C	R	M	P	I	H	E	T
H	C	L	T	W	S	T	Y	L	S
A	W	I	M	U	P	N	R	G	B
R	S	P	I	N	S	S	D	I	S
A	L	Q	S	U	N	S	E	R	S

Word Search

Can you find these eight desert words?

CAMEL
SANDSTORM
CACTUS
MEERKAT
SAHARA
DRY
WINDS
SUN

Amazing Desert Birds

Most birds can fly. Others can run really fast. This helps them search large deserts for water. They get water from the food they eat, too.

Roadrunner

Roadrunners don't fly well. They run along the ground chasing insects, mice, and lizards.

Cactus Wren

These birds make football-shaped nests in cactuses. The cactus provides food and protection.

Gila Woodpecker

This woodpecker makes its nest holes in cactuses. The hole gives it shade and food.

Bearded Vulture

Vultures eat dead animals. If any bones are too big, they drop them from the air to break them!

Ostrich

Ostriches are the largest birds in the world. They can run at 45 miles (70 km) per hour!

Desert Birdwatch

Can you find these birds?

1 ostrich
2 bearded vultures
3 gila woodpeckers
4 roadrunners
5 cactus wrens

Keeping Cool

The heat of the desert in daytime would be too much for most animals. Desert animals have some clever ways to keep cool when they can't find any shade.

Fennec foxes pump blood into their big ears to help keep them cool.

QUESTION

This Cape ground squirrel has a clever way of keeping cool. Can you see what it might be?

Cool Tricks Quiz

Read these two pages. Then, see if you can answer the questions below.

1. What two things do coyotes do to help keep cool?

2. How does a Cape ground squirrel cool down?

3. What gross thing do vultures do to cool themselves?

Cool Meerkats

Meerkats keep cool in daytime in burrows underground. They live in groups. Everyone in the group has a job.

The dark fur around a meerkat's eyes acts like sunglasses—stopping them from getting dazzled by the sun.

Lost Pup!

This pup has gotten lost. Can you help it find the others?

Incredible Diggers

Some desert animals are amazing diggers. Aardvarks have large front claws. They can dig down 1 foot (30 cm) in less than 8 seconds! They dig to find food. They catch termites and ants using their long, sticky tongues.

Find the Hidden Digger

Draw each square into the correct square in the grid below. What amazing digger did you draw?

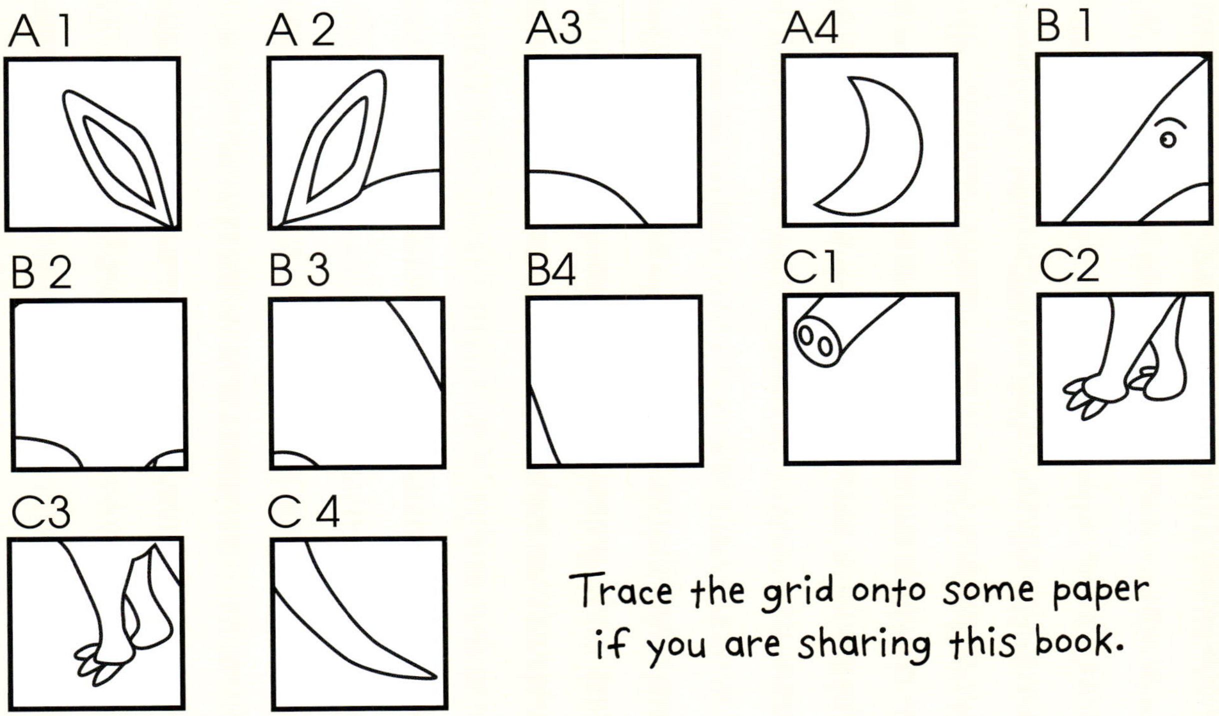

Trace the grid onto some paper if you are sharing this book.

We have filled in the first square for you.

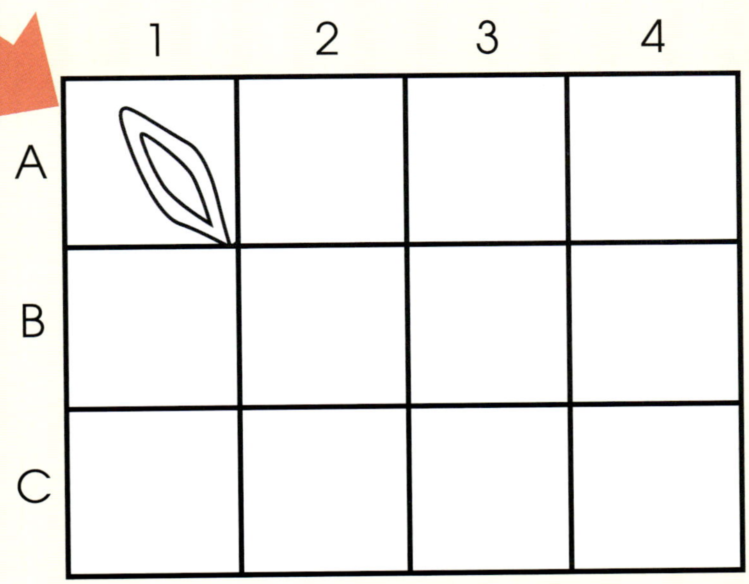

Color It In

Desert Snakes

Like tortoises, cold-blooded snakes can't control their temperature. They warm themselves in the morning sun, then find shade when the sun gets too hot. They sleep underground during the cold winter months, often in big groups.

Snake Match

Can you match the description to the right snake below?

Sidewinders bop up and down along the sand. This means only some of their body touches the hot sand at any one time. Their sandy color helps them hide.

Kingsnakes kill their prey by squeezing. Their skin has red, black, and yellow bands. The bands break up the snake's outline, making it hard for predators to see.

Rattlesnakes have a rattle at the end of their tail. They shake it to scare away predators. Diamondback rattlesnakes are brown with a diamond pattern.

How many snakes are sheltering from the sun in this burrow? With such a snake tangle, try counting the heads.

How Cool Is Shade?

You will need: two shallow bowls, water, a sunny day, a thermometer if you have one

1. Place one bowl in sunshine and the other in the shade.

2. Pour the same amount of water into each bowl.

3. After an hour, dip your finger in each bowl or take the temperature using the thermometer. Which bowl has the warmest water? Did the shade keep it cooler?

If you leave the bowls for a day, some of the water will disappear. Where do you think the water went?

Brilliant Beetles

Beetles are superhero insects! One-third of all animals on Earth are beetles. Their hard outer skeleton protects them from extreme weather and from predators. Most have wings and can fly from danger. Many release a foul-tasting liquid that puts off predators, too!

Beetles are insects. Count this beetle's legs. How many legs do insects have?

Playing Possum

The blue death feigning beetle can't fly or produce smelly liquid. It has another clever way to avoid being eaten. When it is scared, it rolls onto its back and plays dead! Spiders and other predators prefer to eat live prey, so this trick usually works.

The Beetle Game

You will need: a die, a pen or pencil, some paper

Take turns rolling the die. Look at the chart on the right. The number you rolled allows you to draw that part of your beetle.

BUT, you must draw the body first, and then the head, before you can draw the other parts. If the number matches a part that cannot be drawn, or has already been drawn, your turn ends.

When you complete your beetle, shout "Beetle!" The first one to complete their beetle is the winner.

6 — draw the body
5 — draw the head
4 — draw one wing
3 — draw one leg
2 — draw one antenna
1 — draw one eye

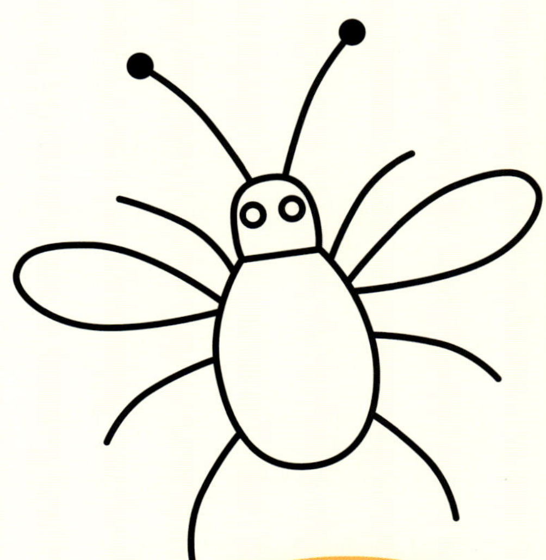

Who'd Eat a Scorpion?

Desert scorpions are fierce hunters. They quickly grab a passing insect or spider with their sharp pincers. They arch their tail forward and sting their prey with its poisonous tip. Then, they rip their prey into pieces using their strong jaws. Some scorpion poison can kill a man.

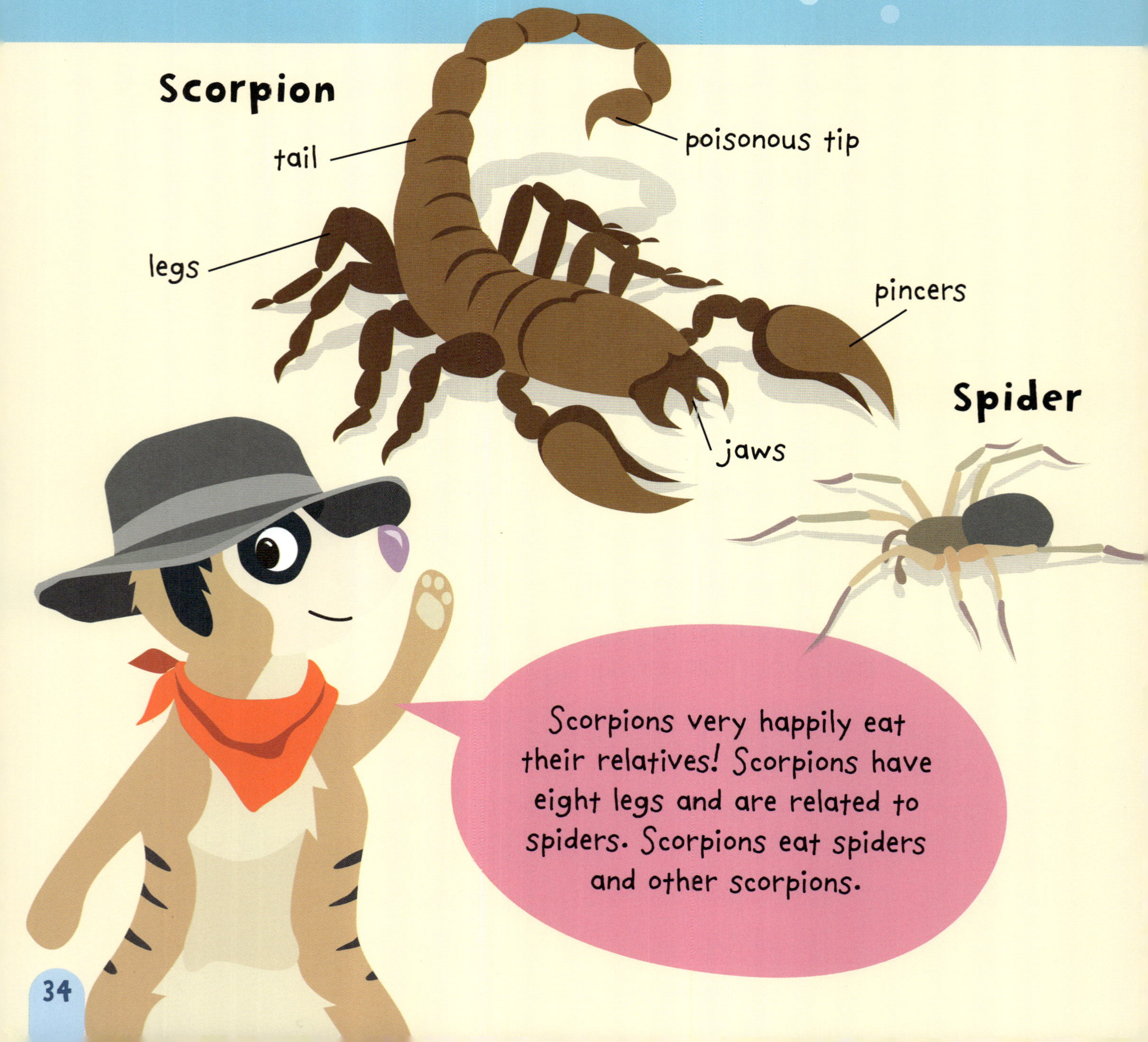

Who'd eat a scorpion? A meerkat would! Meerkats watch and wait until they are sure they can grab the scorpion's tail. They bite off its stinger. They drag the scorpion along the sand to wipe off any poison. Then they eat the scorpion. Meerkats eat spiders, too.

Food Web

A food web is a diagram that shows which animals are food for other animals. Now that you know all about scorpions, meerkats, and spiders, which of these food webs is correct?

Desert Lizards

Lizards are reptiles. Their dry skin is covered with scales or bony plates. Reptiles are cold-blooded, have backbones, and usually lay soft-shelled eggs. Because they can't control their temperature, they usually live in warm places, such as deserts.

The huge Gila monster has a poisonous bite.

Its bright blotches of pink, orange, or yellow warn other animals to stay away.

Gila Monster

Geckos shed their tails if a predator grabs them.

Geckos use their tails to help balance them as they climb.

Lizards store fat in their tails.

Geckos have tiny hairs on their feet that help them grip as they climb.

Gecko

Thorny Devil

G	E	C	K	O	C	F	E	M	P
T	I	P	N	S	H	B	G	N	C
E	U	L	I	Z	A	R	D	C	O
L	F	R	D	T	M	E	R	H	E
Y	A	N	T	S	E	O	R	M	S
J	D	C	R	L	L	K	H	E	T
H	X	L	T	Z	E	T	A	J	S
P	W	I	M	U	O	N	L	N	B
R	I	G	U	A	N	A	D	I	S
A	L	Q	R	T	G	S	E	R	S

Word Search

Can you find these six desert reptiles?

GECKO
SNAKE
LIZARD
IGUANA
CHAMELEON
TURTLE

Clever Cheeks

What does a desert animal do if it finds more food than it can carry? Hamsters and kangaroo rats have a cunning way to carry extra food!

Hamster

Hamsters live in many deserts around the world.

Hamsters carry food in their cheek pouches.

Hamsters' backs are the same color as their surroundings.

Their underside fur is often pale to reflect back heat from the sand.

Kangaroo Rat

Kangaroo rats live in the deserts of North America.

They can live their whole lives never needing water!

Kangaroo rats store food in their cheek pouches.

Their strong back legs help them escape predators.

Where's My Storage Cupboard?

This hamster forgot where he buried his food. Follow the instructions below. Can you help him find the right square on the map?

= move forward   = turn to right   = turn to left

Start

Use tracing paper if you're sharing this book.

Desert Big Cats

Mountain lions are the fourth-largest cat in the world. They are also known as cougars, panthers, or pumas. They live in deserts and other habitats.

Scientists call mountain lions "small cats" because they don't roar! Big cats, such as lions, have a special bone in their throat that lets them make a roaring sound.

Color It In

- 1 = light blue
- 2 = yellow
- 3 = light brown
- 4 = brown
- 5 = pink
- 6 = light gray
- 7 = dark gray
- 8 = green

Copy this picture and then color it in if you are sharing this book.

Colder Deserts

The rocky Gobi desert is on the border between Mongolia and China. It is hot in summer, but in winter the temperature can be as low as -40°F (-40°C).

Golden eagles survive by hunting small mammals, insects, and reptiles. They also pick at the remains of dead animals.

Mongolian wild asses dig with their hooves to reach underground water.

The two-humped Bactrian camels live in the Gobi desert. They grow thick fur to keep warm in winter. They shed this coat in summer.

A camel's humps change size depending on how much fat it has stored. A drooping hump means the camel is running out of fuel.

Connect the Dots to see if this camel needs food.

Use tracing paper or copy the picture if you are sharing this book with others.

Color It In

Desert Name Scramble

Unscramble these words to find the desert names. Write your answers on a separate sheet of paper.

1. ARAHSA ___ ___ ___ ___ ___ ___
2. BIGO ___ ___ ___ ___
3. IRCTATCAN ___ ___ ___ ___ ___ ___ ___ ___ ___

Desert Genius Test

Are you a desert biome genius? Answer these desert questions to find out.

1 What is a desert?

a) Somewhere that gets lots of rain.

b) Somewhere that gets very little rain.

2 Which desert animal would eat a poisonous scorpion?

a) a meerkat

b) a spider

c) a camel

3 Where do camels store food as fat?

a) in their burrows

b) in their cheeks

c) in their humps

4 What desert snake bounces as it moves, so it hardly touches the hot sand?

a) a rattlesnake

b) a sidewinder

c) a kingsnake

5 A kangaroo rat can live its whole life without ever drinking.

a) true   b) false

6 Why do deserts sometimes flood?

a) They don't.

b) Water can't soak into the sandy soil.

c) Deserts get more rain than most places.

Answers

Page 4:

Page 9: b and d. They are both fish.

Page 9 bottom: The rock casts a cooling shadow.

Page 11: a dorcas gazelle

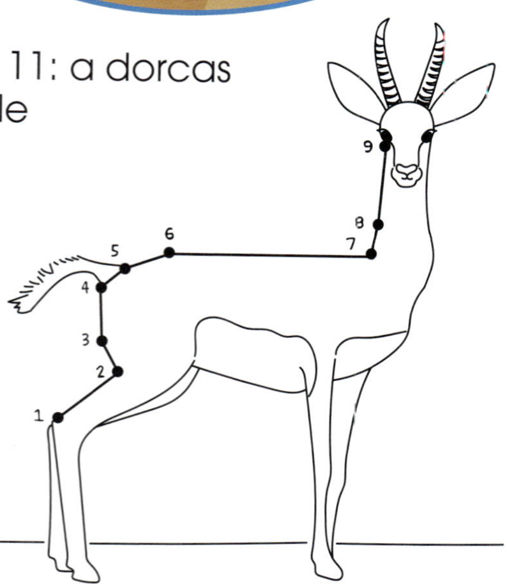

Page 13:

Page 15: The eggs have to turn into toadlets quickly before the puddle dries up.

Page 15 bottom:

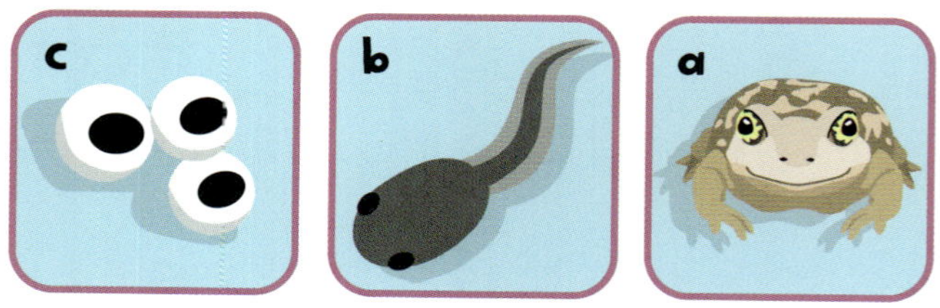

Page 19: 1) e, 2) d, 3) b, 4) c, 5) a

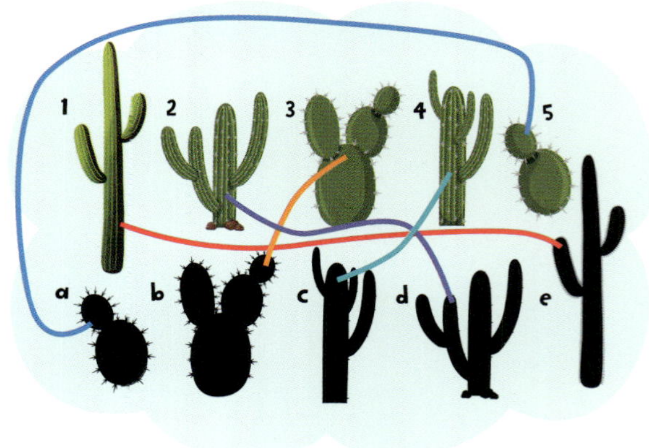

Page 21:

W	E	T	A	K	R	E	E	M	E
L	I	P	N	S	G	B	U	L	C
E	S	N	R	N	C	X	R	C	R
C	F	E	D	T	H	E	R	A	E
S	A	N	D	S	T	O	R	M	S
A	D	C	R	M	P	I	H	E	T
H	C	L	T	W	S	T	Y	L	S
A	W	I	M	U	P	N	R	G	B
R	S	P	I	N	S	S	D	I	S
A	L	Q	S	U	N	S	E	R	S

Page 23:

Page 25: 1) Coyotes pant and lose some fur to keep cool. 2) Cape ground squirrels shelter under the shade of their own tails. 3) Vultures pee on their legs to keep cool.

Page 23:

Page 29: an aardvark

Page 30:

Page 31: There are 10 snakes.

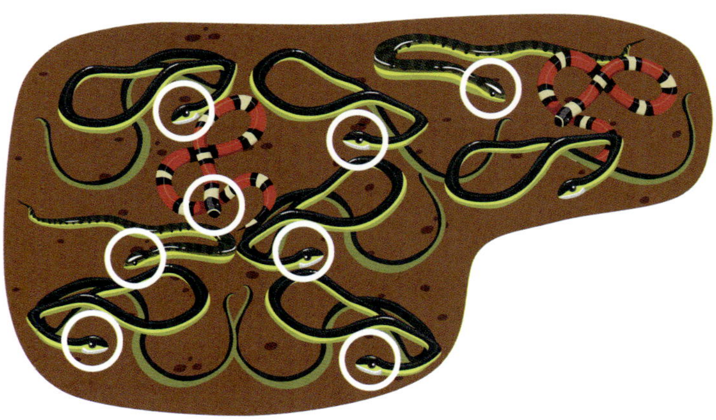

Page 31 bottom: The water will have dried up into the warm air. This is known as evaporation.

Page 32: Insects have six legs.

Page 35: Food web b is correct.

Page 37:

G	E	C	K	O	C	F	E	M	P
T	I	P	N	S	H	B	G	N	C
E	U	L	I	Z	A	R	D	C	O
L	F	R	D	T	M	E	R	H	E
Y	A	N	T	S	E	O	R	M	S
J	D	C	R	L	L	K	H	E	T
H	X	L	T	Z	E	T	A	J	S
P	W	I	M	U	O	N	L	N	B
R	I	G	U	A	N	A	D	I	S
A	L	Q	R	T	G	S	E	R	S

Page 39:

Page 41:

Page 43: The camel needs food.

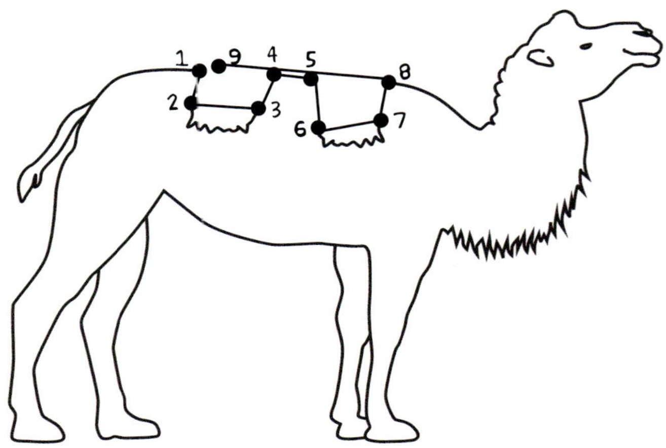

Page 43 bottom: 1) Sahara, 2) Gobi, 3) Antarctic

Page 44: 1) b - Somewhere that gets very little rain. 2) a - A meerkat would eat a scorpion. 3) c - Camels store fat in their humps. 4) b - A sidewinder snake bounces as it moves across the sand. 5) a - True, a kangaroo rat can live its whole life without ever drinking. 6) b - Deserts can flood because water can't soak into the sandy soil.